STOP TY

Write Better
Speech Recognition
(Speech-to-Text Software)

Keith Connes

Copyright © 2018 by Keith Connes. Revised edition.
Published worldwide by Butterfield Press
Cover by Dale Ziemianski

Contents

Introduction

Do you write articles, books, plays, speeches? Or do you use your computer mainly for writing emails? Or something else?

No matter what kind of writing you do, if you're still creating it by typing on a keyboard, I'm going to show you a way to make your writing easier and better. It's called speech recognition or voice typing. That's right, you just speak and a computer program will transcribe your spoken words directly onto your computer. This will be in the form of text you can easily place in a document, email, and even on Facebook or Twitter!

I'm a professional writer and I've been using this speech recognition technology for 20 years. The earlier programs were rather clunky and their transcriptions were not very accurate. But today's programs are so advanced that I hardly ever use the keyboard.

What's more, the particular program I use has a terrific function that allows me to dictate into a compact digital recorder anywhere I happen to be, and then I can upload my dictation into my computer for automatic transcription into text.

Speech recognition not only makes my writing easier, but I've become far more productive. For example, the words you are reading right now were originally spoken into my little digital recorder as I reclined comfortably in an easy chair looking out on a beautiful lake that borders on my property.

So I can write anytime and almost anywhere – relaxing, taking a walk, in a doctor's waiting room, even while driving.

Not surprisingly, I'm a real convert to voice typing and in this book I'm happy to tell you how you can use this terrific technology to make your own writing easier and better. The book is an updated version of *Dragon Naturally Speaking 13 & Professional Individual 13 Handbook for Writers.*

Although some parts of this new updated edition continue to offer ideas that will be of special interest to writers, I have expanded it to make it useful to anyone who uses a computer. I've included details on three *free* speech recognition programs and I compare them to the Dragon programs that are available for purchase.

Depending on the kind of writing you do, one of the free programs might be all you need. On the other hand, one of the Dragon programs might be well worth the price – but which one? This book contains the information, along with my recommendations, that will help you decide.

Also in this book are tips on getting comfortable with dictation, product reviews on useful accessories, and more.

Let's get started.

Overview of the Speech Recognition Programs

There are four providers of personal-use speech recognition programs that I'm aware of. One of them – Nuance's Dragon – costs money, two are totally free, and the fourth is free but with a string attached. In the pages that follow, I'll provide information and commentary on each of the programs. My long-term experience with Dragon products has enabled me to provide, in this book, considerably detailed information that will help you decide whether these sophisticated programs are worth their cost (and a steeper learning curve on your part) versus the simpler free programs.

Free versus Dragon. In addition to being free, the no-cost programs have a major convenience advantage over Dragon: The Dragon programs require each user to create an individual user profile. For Dragon NaturallySpeaking you create your user profile by dictating about five minutes of prepared text while the program analyzes your voice and mic characteristics in order to optimize accuracy. Dragon Professional Individual needs to analyze the mic characteristics only and therefore the user profile is created in less than a minute.

By contrast, the free programs don't have user profiles, so you and anyone else in your household can quickly and easily participate in "voice typing," as Google calls it. In addition, you can conduct interviews or other dialogues using the free programs, whereas Dragon is limited to one user at a time.

In Dragon's favor are its powerful features — many of which I will explain throughout this book. Dragon might be your best option, particularly if you do a lot of writing now or plan to do more in the future. One feature that I consider especially useful is the ability to dictate anywhere into a compatible recorder, upload that dictation into your computer and, after a few mouse clicks and a short waiting period, your recorded dictation will be automatically transcribed into written text.

Much more on that later, but for now, note that the ability to upload recorded dictation into your computer is available in Dragon NaturallySpeaking 13 Premium and Professional Individual 15, but not in the lower-priced Dragon Home editions and also not in any of the free programs.

Dragon Anywhere. This is Nuance's separate cloud-based subscription service that allows you to dictate and edit documents of any length using your iOS or Android device. I am not reviewing Dragon Anywhere in this book, but you can see it demonstrated in a YouTube video titled, *Nuance Dragon Speech Recognition*. You can get a 7-day free trial at nuance.com. The cost of a subscription is $14.99 per month or $149.99 per year.

Dictation Strategies

Getting comfortable with dictating. If you can talk, you can dictate. Imagine that you're having coffee with a friend and you're telling him or her about a great idea you have for a writing project. You are enthusiastic and you're able to articulate that idea in great detail. In fact, you like your idea so much you could talk about it for several hours, or at least until your friend's eyes glaze over. Then the time comes when you have to go to the computer and put it in writing. Now it becomes work. What you had expressed so fluently as you were talking about it has to be re-created word by word, sentence by sentence, at the keyboard.

But wait – instead of going through that, suppose you talk into a microphone and let a speech recognition program do the typing for you. With a little practice, your ideas – and even your finished text – will flow more freely and your project will get done sooner.

If you're not experienced at dictating, at first it may seem to be more intimidating than the familiar keyboard, but you will very likely overcome any discomfort by consistent usage. The main way to get comfortable with dictating is to forget about the microphone and pretend that you are still talking to that friend. Don't worry about speaking in perfectly constructed prose – just relax and talk. If your sentences come out fragmented and your word choices are not always the best, you can edit them into shape later, using the mic or the keyboard or both.

In the beginning, avoid the temptation of watching your words appear on the screen as you dictate. Seeing any mistakes emerge in black and white as you utter them can be very discouraging and can interrupt the flow of your dictation. Also, start by dictating something that doesn't require a lot of thought. In other words, start with small, easy steps – as you would when beginning any learning activity – to allow your self-confidence and competence to develop with minimal setbacks.

Tip: Don't lose your momentum when you make corrections. If you're in the middle of a sentence and you think of a better way to say it, simply say "correction," re-state the sentence, and clean it up afterwards. That way, your train of thought will keep chugging down the track. And give yourself permission to ramble! If an idea for another project, or another part of the project you're working on, occurs to you while you're dictating, just say something like, "Note, add a paragraph on shopping for bulletproof vests in *Vacationing in Syria*." Then, when you see that note in the transcribed dictation, you can move it to where it belongs.

If it would help you to become relaxed with dictating, consider simply turning on a recorder while you're talking to that friend about your project and you can then transform your recorded words into a written document.

The main thing is to stay with the dictation process and allow it to become familiar and comfortable. And if you're using Dragon, don't get bogged down in the beginning with its many commands. Although I have used Dragon for years I still make value judgments during the editing process as to which spoken commands I use versus keyboard and mouse.

Testing the Free Programs

To help evaluate the accuracy of these programs I dictated into each program a test paragraph that included an unusual name (mine), and address, a dollar amount, a company name, another number, and various types of punctuation including a couple of dashes. The test paragraph appears below in bold type.

My name is Keith Connes and I live at 1029 Riverview St., Cincinnati, OH. I think Ohio is a very nice state. On one of the farms near me, the field workers are paid $10.25 an hour. There is a company in town called Brown & Sons that has been in business for 125 years! But there are other companies – even older ones – in the same town. Isn't that interesting?

I began by dictating the paragraph using Dragon and it transcribed the text just as you see it, without any mistakes. Notice, for example, that when I dictated an address, Dragon recognized it as such, inserted commas in the right place, and typed the abbreviation "OH." Then, when I mentioned Ohio again in a narrative form, Dragon typed its full name. For the dollar figure, I dictated "ten dollars and twenty-five cents" and the Dragon transcribed that in the customary format. Same with "one hundred twenty-five." For the company name, I dictated "cap brown ampersand cap sons." (Dragon interprets "cap" as the command to capitalize.) Each time I said "dash" I got a dash sign, including a space before and after it. I ended the paragraph by saying "question mark." By the way, my last name is unusual and is commonly mispronounced, but it was easy to teach Dragon to recognize it and properly spell it. (I wish *people* would do the same!) Also by the way, I don't live at the Cincinnati address – I just made it up.

Note that although Dragon transcribed the test paragraph perfectly, it does make mistakes from time to time. Fortunately, there are ways to train it to reduce its mistakes.

You'll see how each of the free programs handled the test paragraph in the evaluations that follow

Windows Speech Recognition

This program is built right into the Windows operating system. To open it, click on the search bar on the left-hand side of your taskbar. A Cortana menu will appear. Click on Apps. In the Apps menu, click on Speech Recognition. A screen will appear at the top with either the word "Listening" or "Sleeping" in the field to the right of the mic icon. If it's "Sleeping," say "start listening" and that will turn the mic on. When you want to turn the mic off, say "stop listening" and the mic will go into sleeping mode.

'You can dictate into WordPad or a blank Word and then copy and paste your text wherever you want it. And your dictation can include punctuation marks, such as **? ! / \ # & @ *** by saying their names, i.e., "question mark," "exclamation point," "forward slash," etc. If you want the descriptive word(s) to appear instead of the punctuation mark, you can say, for example, "literal question mark" and the words "question mark" will appear instead of the "?" punctuation. For a more complete list, Google "Windows Speech Recognition Commands" .

To exit the program, click on the "X" in the mic display's upper-right corner. Now here's how Windows Speech Recognition transcribed my test paragraph:

My name is Keith Connes and I live at 1029 river view street Cincinnati Ohio. I think Ohio is a very nice state. On one of the farms near me, the field workers are paid $10.25 an hour. There is any company in town called cap brown & Ons that has been in business for a 125 years! But there are other companies dashed even older ones – in the same town. Isn't that interesting?

Not bad. Somewhat to my surprise, the program spelled my name correctly and I did not teach it to do that because, to be honest, I don't know that there's a way to teach it. The street address needs some editing. "a company" was transcribed as "any company, and trying to capitalize the name "Brown" simply resulted in the words "cap" and "brown." The word I had dictated as "Sons" did get capitalized but it was spelled incorrectly. The phrase "for 125 years had an unwanted "a" inserted, but I've had that even with Dragon and it might be due to imperfect dictation on my part. My first attempt at a dash got "dashed" but I got a real dash the second time.

I think that's a pretty good job of transcription for a free program with no training.

If the program is uncertain about a word or phrase you dictated, a menu will appear with a numbered lists of possibilities. If you see the one you want, say its number, followed by "OK." If you don't see it, close the menu and start typing.

My evaluation: This program has a lot of good features but it made a lot of mistakes when I used it more extensively than the test paragraph. For example, "you see" kept appearing as "UC" no matter how carefully I pronounced it. And it does not appear to learn from repeated corrections. For example, when I tried to dictate "mic," the abbreviation for "microphone," I consistently got "Mike." Yes, the two words sound exactly alike, but a sophisticated program like Dragon can be taught to come up with the desired word, at least most of the time. Granted, it's not a lot of trouble to change "Mike" into "mic" during the editing process – and you will need to do some editing with *any* speech recognition program – but when I used it more extensively the Windows program transcribed a lot of words and phrases that were quite different from what I was dictating, so be prepared for considerable editing if you want your finished product to make sense.

Google Voice Typing

To use this program, you must have Google Chrome as a browser. You can download it at google.com/chrome. When you're ready to dictate, activate Google Voice Typing by opening Chrome and clicking on the Apps icon – a square made up of nine dots, located at the upper left and/or upper right of the toolbar. From the Apps menu that appears, select the icon labeled "Docs." (If you don't see it, click on "More" and when you finally see "Docs," you can drag it to the top row of the Apps icons for future use.)

Clicking on "Docs" will take you to the home page of Google's word processing program called, yes, Google Docs. (You might be required to create a free Google account if you don't have one.) From the row of templates, click on the blank template or any other template you want to use. Then, from the **Tools** drop-down menu, select **Voice Typing**. A black mic icon will appear at the upper left. Click on it and it will turn red, indicating that you can start dictating. To turn the mic off, click on its icon again. Depending on what you want to do with your dictation, you can remain in Docs, which is similar to Microsoft Word, or you can copy and paste the text into another location, such as a Word file or an email message.

Now here's how Google Voice Typing transcribed my text paragraph:

My name is Keith, and I live at 1029 Riverview Street Cincinnati Ohio. I think Ohio is a very nice State. On one of the farms near me, the field workers are paid $10.25 an hour. There is a company in town called CAP Brown Ampersand guns that has been in the business for 125 years! But there are other companies - even older ones that in the same town. Isn't that interesting?

Okay, Google Voice Typing transcribed my last name as a comma, which is fairly close, – as the name is pronounced CONN-ness. The street address is also pretty close, but not punctuated properly. Notice that "State" is capitalized for no good reason, and the program has randomly capitalized words at other times, so that seems to be an ongoing glitch. "Brown & Sons" did not work out very well. Also, I got one almost-dash (a hyphen) and the second attempted dash was transcribed as "that." Still, a fairly good job of transcribing.

My evaluation: I found this program to be somewhat limited, with a number of annoying traits. Among the limitations are the punctuation commands. The good news is, you can successfully dictate such punctuation commands as **period, comma, exclamation point, and question mark**. The bad news is, if you dictate **open/close parenthesis, colon, semicolon, ampersand, pound sign,** or **asterisk**, the program will simply type these commands as words, which is not what you want.

Among the annoying traits, the mic icon is likely to turn off if you've paused in your dictation for a short period of time, requiring you to click it back on with exasperating frequency. Another of the program's eccentricities is a tendency to randomly bunch two words together without a space in between.

There is an extensive Help menu that can be accessed by clicking on a question mark that appears when you place your cursor in the lower right corner of the mic icon when it is off. Regrettably, some of the Help instructions – for example, voice commands to place the cursor where you want it – don't all work as advertised.

Microsoft Garage Dictate

The software giant has a corporate endeavor it calls Microsoft Garage, wherein a number of fortunate employees are allowed to develop software they are passionate about. One of these projects is the free speech recognition program called "Dictate." The term "Garage" indicates that it is a work in progress and might be blessed with major improvements over time.

It is said to be currently available only to users of Office 360, a.k.a. Office 2016. If you have that version, you can download Dictate by typing "dictate.ms" into your browser. If that doesn't work, try "dictate.azurewebsites.net."

To activate the program after it has been downloaded, open a Word document or an Outlook outgoing email. You'll see a new tab labeled "Dictation." Click on it and a mic icon will appear at the upper left of your screen with the word "Start" beneath it. If you want to dictate your own punctuation (recommended), click on the button labeled "Manual Punctuation," then click on the mic icon to open it, and start dictating. To turn the mic off, click on its icon again.

Here's the way the Microsoft program transcribed my test paragraph:

My name is Keith Kanis. And I live at. 1029 Riverview St. Cincinnati Ohio. I think Ohio is a very nice state. . On one of the farms near me, the field workers are paid $10.25 an hour period. There is a company in town called? Cap Brown ampersand Cap sonsThat has been in business for 125 years! But there are other companies dash even older ones dash in the same town. Isn't that interesting?

Nice try on my second name – I really didn't expect much better. There were some unwanted periods and one that was spelled out. "Brown & Sons" will need a lot of editing. Although the dash command did not work in this dictation, in another session the program gave me a hyphen. Which brings up the following point: None of the programs (including free and Dragon) is completely consistent, meaning that sometimes you will get what you dictated and sometimes you won't. Careful proofreading is always on the menu.

With Dictate, you can say the commands **new line, new paragraph,** and the following punctuation marks: **period, comma, question mark, exclamation point/mark, colon,** and **semicolon.** Unfortunately, **open/close parenthesis** cannot be dictated. Worse yet, you can't even capitalize with a command and I could not discover any commands that would move the cursor.

One feature that might be very handy for some users is the program's ability to translate dictation from English into a multitude of other languages or vice versa. For example, if you select English to French, you can say "I love you" and the program will type "je t'aime."

So...which program? As you can see from their descriptions, the free programs offer several benefits. For one thing, they are free, so your only commitment is the time you'll spend becoming familiar with whichever program (or programs) you decide to try. Also, you can start dictating with any of them almost immediately because they don't require training and they are not restricted to an individual user – anyone in your household can quickly use these voice-to-text programs.

The challenge will be to get a high degree of accuracy from the program of your choice and to learn how to use its features pretty much on your own. However, there are some tutorials provided by various individuals on YouTube (search by program name, such as Google Voice Typing or simply "speech to text") and I encourage you to watch them. I also encourage you to try one or more of the free program as well.

Given that you can use one or more of these three free speech recognition programs, why spend money for a Dragon program – especially when it requires each person who uses it to have his or her own user profile?

The answer lies partly in the kinds of use you will have for the program and also the degree of sophistication and overall competence you expect. If you're looking for the greatest accuracy – and particularly if you can see the value in dictating anywhere into a small digital recorder and easily uploading that dictation for transcription – you might find that Dragon is well worth its cost and effort.

I'll tell you much more about Dragon in the pages that follow, so I invite you to read – and then decide.

Dragon NaturallySpeaking 13 Premium

As I mentioned earlier, I've been using Dragon software for 20 years, moving from one upgrade to the next, and I was pleased with the results I was getting from NaturallySpeaking 13 Premium. I was really disappointed to learn that its manufacturer, Nuance, has stopped selling this capable product, stating as follows:

"Nuance Communications is updating its line of Dragon Professional and Consumer desktop speech recognition solutions with a simplified selection to better meet the needs of home-based consumers, professional individuals, and enterprise customers …

"Customers who have purchased Dragon Premium 13 own a perpetual license to the solution and may continue using it. Nuance will no longer provide updates for the solution after January 1, 2019, however support will continue 90 days from activation."

The above information – as well all other Dragon-related contents in this book – refers to Dragon products for PC. However, Nuance has since announced the immediate discontinuance of production and support of *all* Dragon products for Mac.

Nuance has introduced Home 15, an upgrade of the NaturallySpeaking Home edition. Unfortunately, their Home editions lack the ability to transcribe recorded dictation – a really useful feature of NaturallySpeaking 13 Premium and Nuance's more expensive Professional Individual 15. Therefore, I am having a hard time understanding how the discontinuance of

NaturallySpeaking 13 Premium without a direct replacement in its price range will, in the words of Nuance, "better meet the needs of home-based consumers."

Happily, at this writing, third-party sources such as Amazon and eBay are continuing to sell NaturallySpeaking 13 Premium at very attractive prices. Therefore, I have included an updated report on this useful software. Also, I'll share some workarounds I've developed to deal with Dragon's imperfections.

Although this is not intended to be a comprehensive user manual, I've provided many operating details in order to give you a good idea of what it's like to work with Dragon. For example, I describe the training process that enables Dragon to adapt to the characteristics of your speech and your mic, as well as various ways you can add words and proper names that are not in Dragon's vocabulary. Incidentally, these operating procedures are similar to those of the more expensive Professional Individual 15, which has additional features of its own. For more details, see my review of this program later in this book.

Creating user profiles. As soon as you install Dragon you will be prompted to create a user profile and a Wizard will take you through the necessary steps. The process will take about five minutes. When you're finished, you will name this profile and that name will reside in the Profile tab of the DragonBar (described below). If you also use another type of mic, such as a wireless in addition to a plug-in, and/or a recorder, it's advisable to train Dragon to adapt to each source's sound characteristics – although this process is somewhat simplified in Professional Individual 15.

The DragonBar – New vs Classic. The DragonBar is a control center you'll use for such functions as turning the mic on and off, selecting a user profile, opening the DragonPad or the Dictation Box (more about them later), customizing Dragon's vocabulary, and much more. You can get around easily by means of pull-down menus. The DragonBar is available in two styles – New and Classic. When you install either NaturallySpeaking 13 or Professional Individual 15/2, the New DragonBar will appear by default. You can switch back and forth between the New DragonBar and the Classic DragonBar, which is a holdover from earlier versions of NaturallySpeaking. Both styles provide pretty much the same options, the major difference being their appearance and the way they take up real estate on your screen. Of the two, the New DragonBar is narrower and fatter, but it also has an optional Auto-collapse function that will cause it to shrink to a very small footprint until you place your cursor on it. The New DragonBar will also show definitions of certain options when you click on them.

The Classic DragonBar runs across the entire top of the screen with a choice of two depths, depending on how much information you want to see. You might want to try both the New and Classic styles to determine which one you prefer.

Punctuate as you dictate. You can use various commands to create punctuation. If you want to capitalize a word within a sentence, say "cap" immediately followed by the word. (Suppose you want to use the word "cap" in a sentence? I'll get to that later.) If you want to capitalize more than one word, for example, the title of a play, say "caps on The Man Who Came to Dinner." Note that the word "to" will not be capitalized, in accordance with accepted grammatical usage.

Be sure to remember to say "caps off" when you are through with the phrase or Dragon will continue to capitalize each word you subsequently dictate. This happens to me more often than I would like to admit and I Discover a Whole Bunch of Words Such As These That I Did Not Want Capitalized. I fix that by selecting that text and then pressing the Shift and F3 keys twice. (Pressing Shift and F3 once at that point would result in ALL CAPS.) To capitalize an entire word, say "all caps" followed by the word. To capitalize two or more consecutive words, say "all caps on" and to stop the capitalization, say "all caps off." Similarly, you can avoid caps entirely with the command "no caps."

To enclose a phrase in quotation marks, say "open quotes" at the beginning and "close quotes" at the end. For parentheses, use "open paren" and "close paren." To hyphenate a series of words, say them without pauses, then, after a brief pause, give the command "hyphenate that." For example, say "one of a kind" (brief pause) "hyphenate that" and it will appear as "one-of-a-kind." Sometimes a command won't do its job, but will appear instead as text, for example, "one of a kind hyphenate that." The probable cause is that you didn't pause the right length of time, according to Dragon's tastes, for the command to be recognized as such. Eventually, you'll get the timing right, but maybe not always. At least, I don't always get it right. (More on this subject later on.)

"New paragraph" versus "new line." For some reason, when you say the command "new paragraph," Dragon enters two lines, as if you had pressed Enter twice. If you want to start a new paragraph on the very next line, that is, as if you had pressed Enter only once, say "new line." First, however, you will have to make a one-time change. By default, the first word of the new line will be in lower case (unless it is normally capitalized, such "Robert" or the subject pronoun "I"). To have any beginning word of a new line automatically capitalized, go to **DragonBar/Vocabulary/Vocabulary Editor**. Change the **Display** drop-down list to **Words with spoken forms only**, search for **new line**, click on **properties** and from the drop-down list **Format the next word** choose **capitalized**.

Dictating "period" as a word. Whenever Dragon hears the word "period" it assumes that this is a command to end the sentence, insert a period as punctuation, and start a new sentence with its first word capitalized. Thus, if you dictate "This was the best period in my life" chances are it will be transcribed as "This was the best. In my life." Not quite what you intended. Pressing the Shift key as you say the word "period" is supposed to bypass the command function, but it frequently doesn't work. Using the Correction Menu for this purpose does work but it is time-consuming.

So, what to do? You have several choices. One is to type the word "period" instead of dictating it. However, if you plan to use "period" frequently in your document, or you are dictating away from the keyboard, here is a technique you can use in a variety of situations: Dictate a unique substitute word and then use Word's Find and Replace function. For example, you could say, "This was the best coconut in my life" then use Find and Replace (Alt e,e) to replace each use of "coconut" with "period" – provided, of course, you are not writing about coconuts, in which case it would be advisable to choose a different word.

A third method, which requires you to be at the computer, is to say the word "spell" as a command, followed *immediately* by spelling the word "period ." Thus, to dictate "This was the best period in my life," say "This was the best spell p-e-r-i-o-d in my life." Don't pause for even a split second between "spell" and "p-e-r-i-o-d." A Spelling Window will appear, listing a number of choices, probably with "period" has the first choice, in which case you will say "Choose One." This method is also good when there are words that sound alike, such as "sense" and "cents" and you want to be sure that Dragon makes the right choice.

Caution: You might try to outfox Dragon by entering "period" as a new word in the program's vocabulary, in which case you'll likely lose "period" as a punctuation command. The workaround to *that* workaround is to say "full stop" instead of "period" at the end of your sentences.

Of course, you can use one of the above procedures for other commands – for example, when you want to dictate the word "cap" as part of your text and not as a capitalization command. So instead of dictating "I bought a beautiful cap today" – which Dragon will frequently transcribe as "I bought a beautiful Today" – say "I bought a beautiful coconut today" (or any other word that you won't otherwise use) and later replace each use of it with "cap." Alternatively, say "I bought a beautiful spell c-a-p today, or just type it in."

You can apply the same technique to any word or name that Dragon doesn't recognize and that you'll use a number of times in a document. Let's say it's the name Miklewszki. You could go through the process of adding Miklewszki to Dragon's vocabulary but you might not want to bother if you don't expect to use it in future documents. Instead, dictate, say, Smith (which Dragon already knows) and then, when your dictation is done, Find and Replace all uses of Smith with Miklewszki.

To pause or not to pause. Even if you are an experienced dictator, be aware that when using Dragon there are certain circumstances in which you must be sure to pause and other circumstances in which you must be equally sure *not* to pause, as follows: When you issue a command, such as "delete last three words," you must pause briefly before dictating that command in order for it to take effect. If you do not pause, Dragon will likely assume that the phrase is part of your text and instead of deleting the last three words it will simply type "delete last three words." Likewise, if you were to dictate "6:30 to 8:30" without pausing after "6:30" there's a good chance that Dragon will consider "to" as "2" and will type "6:32 8:30."

On the other hand, suppose you want to write about one of the many trade names that are squished together – for example, GoDaddy. To show the name in that form, add it to Dragon's vocabulary, typing it the way you want it to appear and training the program to hear the two words spoken as if they were one. Alternatively, if you're going to use the name only a few times and don't want to bother training the program, you can simply say, without pausing, "caps on go no space daddy" and you'll get GoDaddy. Remember to then say "caps off." Or say Smith instead and use Find and Replace.

If all of the alternative methods I keep providing seem tiresome, bear in mind that I am trying to help you determine which particular method works best for you.

Transcribing someone else's voice by "parroting."
If you've recorded some speech by someone who has not created a user profile, you can still get Dragon to transcribe it. The method – which is rather work-intensive – is the so-called "parroting" technique, by which you play the speech back through a headset, dictating it as you hear it through the headset. One benefit of parroting is that you can make changes as you go along – for example, you can smooth out grammatical mistakes while at the same time you dictate punctuation commands.

Modes for Dictation. Five modes can be accessed from the DragonBar. Choose the mode that will be most suitable for the type of dictation you plan to do. Here's how each mode functions:

The Dictation & Commands Mode. (On the Classic DragonBar this is called the **Normal Mode**.) You will probably use this mode most of the time because, as its name indicates, it allows you to dictate both text and commands interchangeably.

The Dictation Mode. In this mode, NaturallySpeaking recognizes only such basic commands as "new line" and "new paragraph," as well as such punctuation as "open/close paren," "open/close quotes," "dash," "exclamation point," and "period." Use this mode when you want to dictate as text words that NaturallySpeaking might interpret as commands. For example, suppose you want to dictate, "I was really anxious to correct that unfavorable impression." In the Dictation & Commands Mode, NaturallySpeaking might consider the words "correct that" to be a command and would then open the Correction Menu in the middle of your sentence – not at all what you want – whereas, in the Dictation Mode the entire sentence would be regarded as text. Therefore, it's the safest mode to use when you are dictating text via a Bluetooth or wireless headset and you're not watching the monitor.

The Command Mode. In this mode, NaturallySpeaking responds only to commands and therefore it will not transcribe text. According to NaturallySpeaking's user manual, "This can be helpful when formatting an existing document." Well, I suppose so, but those same commands are available in the Dictation & Commands Mode, which I use to format my documents, because I will invariably want to do some editing and polishing at the same time. Nevertheless, the Command Mode might suit your style of working.

The Numbers Mode. Use this mode when you want NaturallySpeaking to transcribe all numbers in numeral form, as opposed to spelling them out. Note that you can also accomplish this in the Dictation & Commands mode by saying the word "numeral" before you say the number, but if you're dictating a group of numbers it will be easier to use the Numbers Mode.

The Spell Mode. Use this mode to dictate, for example, a name that is not in NaturallySpeaking's vocabulary by spelling it. In this mode, you can also dictate numbers, symbols, and commands.

Now let's look at a couple of "parking spaces" in which you can enter your dictation on a temporary basis:

The DragonPad. Open it at **DragonBar/Tools/DragonPad.** This is a built-in word processor with basic text formatting and editing features. It is similar to Microsoft WordPad, but it is optimized for dictation and has speech recognition features. For example, while using WordPad you can command Dragon to open a file. When you've completed your dictation, copy and paste it into the desired location.

Tip: If you dictate directly into an email program, such as Outlook, and you use the word "send" in a sentence – for example, "Would you please send me a photo of yourself?" – Dragon might interpret "send" as a command, in which case it will promptly send your email to the recipient, right in midsentence! If you find that you are having this problem, there are several workarounds. One is to leave the "To" field blank until you've dictated the entire message. Another is to select the Dictation Mode, which effectively disables commands. And a third method is to dictate your email into DragonPad or the Dictation Box (described shortly), then copy and paste it into the email. As usual, choose whatever works best for you.

Incidentally, Dragon also considers the word "post" as a command to send, and one time I was dictating an email and used the word "boast," which Dragon read as "post" and promptly sent the email. I had not taken my own advice. Lesson learned.

Note that none of the above applies when using Professional Individual 15, which will not send your email until you say "click-send."

The Dictation Box. Open it at **DragonBar/Tools/Dictation Box** or press Control + Shift + D, or simply say "open dictation box." You use the Dictation Box to dictate text and then transfer it to a text field or application. You can dictate commands such as "new line" and "new paragraph" but such file commands as "send" and "open" simply appear as text. The Dictation

Box will open automatically and begin receiving your dictation if you are trying to dictate while you are using an application that is not supported by Dragon.

The first time you open the Dictation Box, click on Settings, then check the box stating "Keep transferred text in the clipboard when the Dictation Box is closed." This will enable you to paste your dictation in the future, as long as it remains in the clipboard.

The Settings mode will also enable you to change the font of the text that appears in the Dictation Box from the default Arial, but that should not be necessary because any text you transfer from the Dictation Box will adopt the font and other formatting characteristics of the document to which it is transferred.

Obviously, another depository for your dictation is a blank document you create in, for example, WordPad or Word. As always, it's a good idea to try various options and then determine what works best for you.

Formatting Text and More

You can literally tell the cursor where to go. For example: "insert before <xyz>" "go to end of line" "go up/down <n> lines or paragraphs" "insert before/after <word or phrase>" "move left/right <n> words/characters." (When commanding the cursor to move left or right a certain number of words, note that Dragon counts a punctuation mark as a word.) For a complete list, go to support.nuance.com and download the cheat sheet for either NaturallySpeaking or Professional Individual. (As of this writing, to get to Professional Individual tutorials you must first click on the NaturallySpeaking link.)

In addition, you can use voice commands to delete or change words or whole lines of text. Using the preceding sentence as an example, if you wanted to change "use voice commands" to "speak instead of type" you would say "select use voice commands," pause until that phrase has been selected, then say "speak instead of type" and the new phrase will replace the old one. You can make text bold by selecting it; for example, say "select beautiful through frustrating" and then say "bold that." If, after seeing the bold text, you decide you liked it better as normal text, say "un-bold that." In the same way, you would say "un-italicize that" and even "un-underline that."

You can use the command "press" instead of physically pressing certain keys on your keyboard – for example, "press control F" to open the Navigation menu in Word; "press escape" for the Esc key; "press enter" for, of course, the Enter key ; "press Windows D" to show your desktop, and many other keys as well.

Then there are the "click" commands that allow you to use your voice instead of the left or right mouse button. For example, if you want to move from the Home tab to the View tab, say "click view." To activate Heading 1, say "click heading one." Note that saying "click" is equivalent to pressing the left mouse button once, while "double-click" is like pressing the left mouse button twice and "right-click" is your verbal substitute for pressing the right mouse button.

Other commands are used specifically in Word and don't need to be preceded by "press" or "click." Here are a few examples: "new file" "save the file." "save file as" "add page numbers" "find a word." "find and replace" "insert a 5 by 8 table" "zoom to 75 percent." "Set page width to 6 inches." You can also dictate various print and color commands and more.

In addition to changing text, Dragon will perform assignments for you. Here are some examples, as listed in Nuance's cheat sheets: "Search the Web for Italian restaurants in Boston." "Search eBay for maternity clothes." "Search Google for 53 divided by 12." "Search video for JFK inaugural address." "Post to Facebook 'Looking forward to a fun night with friends.'"

Obviously, it's up to you to determine which commands you want to perform by voice as opposed to the mouse and keyboard (or touch screen). Regardless, my advice is to make a simple start by dictating text along with a few basic commands, and after you've become comfortable with those procedures, try your hand – or rather, your voice – at other functions.

Automatic formatting. Dragon has functions in **DragonBar/Tools/Auto-Formatting** that can make your dictating life easier. Just make sure the desired boxes are checked in the menu. For example, if **Street addresses** is checked and you dictate "234 main street Santa Barbara California 93110" it will be typed as 234 Main St., Santa Barbara, CA 93110. Other useful categories for auto-formatting include phone numbers, times, and email addresses. One function that I do not care for is **Automatically add commas and periods**. The problem is, sometimes it works and sometimes it doesn't, so to be safe I have unchecked that function and when I want a comma I say "comma" and when I come to the end of a sentence I say "period." This quickly becomes second nature as one gains experience in dictating.

    More options. Click on **DragonBar/ Tools/Options** to see a wide variety of ways in which you can customize Dragon by checking or unchecking boxes. It will take a little time to do this, but it will save a lot of time over the long run.

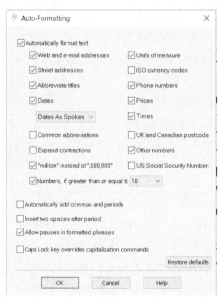

Methods of correcting text: Even after you have trained and repeatedly corrected Dragon it will sometimes make the wrong choices. Take, for example, **two** versus **to**. The program is supposed to know which word to use, based on the context of your dictation – and it usually does, but not always. So let's say you dictated "I want **two** apples" but Dragon has typed "I want **to** apples." You have a couple of options. You could make the correction "the Dragon way" by dictating "correct to."

If there are multiple instances where either "two" or "to" appears in your text, Dragon will superimpose a number over each one. If you want to correct the fifth one, say "choose five." You will then see the **Correction Menu**, which might display the correctly spelled word as your first choice. In that case, say "choose one" and the correction will be made. But if you prefer (as I do), you can program Dragon to always select only the last instance of the misunderstood word, which will usually save you time and effort. From the DragonBar, choose **Tools, Options, Commands** and uncheck **enable multiple text matches,** then click **Apply** and **OK**.

Then there's the old-fashioned way, which I believe will often save even more time and effort: Make the correction with the mouse and keyboard! I have encountered many instances where it is more straightforward to make "hands-on" corrections than dictate a bunch of commands. During the editing process, I often find myself deciding between dictating a Dragon command or reaching for the mouse and keyboard. I'm sure this is highly subjective, but even the Dragon tutorial states, "Just because you can do everything by voice doesn't mean you have to."

Incidentally, another mistake that Dragon often makes (as do real people) is the use of **it's** for **its**. Example: "I saw **it's** potential value." Wrong – it should be "I saw **its** potential value." That's because **it's** is a contraction of **it is**, so if in doubt, mentally substitute **it is** for **it's** and see if it makes sense. You wouldn't say, "I saw **it is** potential value," so obviously you should use **its**, which is the possessive of **it**.

It has been my experience that Dragon does not always learn from even repeated corrections. Perhaps it takes the patience of a kindergarten teacher, and maybe if I made the same correction 20 or 50 times, Dragon would finally get the message. I'm not likely to find out, because after four or five tries, I will sigh, shrug, and resign myself to manually entering the correction. It's the curse of being a Type A person. Your type may vary.

Tip: if Dragon frequently confuses words that sound similar, such as "end" and "and," or "fine" and "find," try emphasizing the correct vowel or consonant a little more strongly during your dictation.

Play back your dictation. There might be times when Dragon transcribes some of your dictation incorrectly and you want to recall exactly what you said. Select the desired text, then click **DragonBar/Audio/Playback**, or simply say "playback," and you'll hear your original dictation. Note that this feature works with text that has been dictated but not text that has been typed.

A variation on playback is text-to-speech. This feature reads text in Dragon's own computer voice. You can use text-to-speech if you are visually impaired or if you just want to have a document read to you. It doesn't have to be something you dictated – the feature will read aloud any Word file, for example, or you could copy material into a text window such as DragonPad to hear it instead of reading it. The computer voice is that of a female speaking quite clearly but understandably devoid of passion – somewhat like the voice in your GPS that tells you to take the next exit on your right. To activate this feature, select the desired text and click on **DragonBar/Audio/Read That** or say "read that." Note that this function reads only printed words, so you cannot use it like playback to determine any discrepancies between your dictation and its transcription by Dragon.

The playback and text-to-speech functions are not available in the Home edition of NaturallySpeaking 13, but playback is included in the new Dragon Home 15, described later in this book.

Adding to Dragon's Vocabulary.

Suppose Dragon doesn't recognize a proper name that you dictate. The program won't just type "Say WHAT?" or "You gotta be kidding!" Rather, it will either do nothing or it will type one or more words that sound like what you're saying. For example, when I first dictated the name of the composer Glazunov, Dragon dutifully typed "clots and of." So here's how to train the program to learn names, words, or even phrases it is misunderstanding: Go to **DragonBar/ Vocabulary/ Add new word or phrase**.

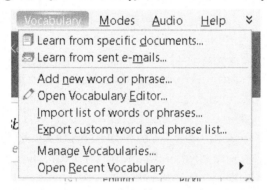

In the first field headed **Spell or type the word(s) to be added** type in your new word or phrase. In the second field headed **Spoken form (if different)** you might have to type in the word or phrase again even if it is *not* different, in order to enable the **Add** button.

After you've filled in both fields, check the box labeled **I want to train the pronunciation of this word or phrase**. Then click **Add** and if you have typed the same word or phrase in both fields sometimes you'll see a screen that warns you "The spoken form you have entered is identical to the written form. This is unnecessary, and the contents of the Spoken form field will be ignored."

Regardless, just click **OK.** The next screen, **Train Words**, will display the word(s) you have typed in and you will be instructed to "Click Go to begin recording your speech**."** Click **Go** and dictate into the mic your chosen word or phrase. Don't over-emphasize your pronunciation – use your normal volume and inflections. When you have finished, click either **Done** or **Done & Train Another**.

You can also use this procedure to create a shortcut, such as your email address. In the first field you would type in your email address exactly as you want it to appear, i.e., "johnsmith@verizon.net" and in the second field you might type in, for example, "email shortcut." Thereafter, Dragon will type in the complete email address whenever it hears "email shortcut." Be aware that if you choose a shortcut such as "my email" the program will type your email address even if you have inadvertently activated the shortcut by dictating "I hope you received my email." So choose a shortcut you will remember but one that you are not likely to use as part of a sentence.

You can see all the words, as well as symbols, that are currently in Dragon's vocabulary by looking them up in **DragonBar/Vocabulary/Open Vocabulary Editor**. A search function will quickly get you to whatever you're looking for. While there, you can also make changes and additions.

Another way of adding words to Dragon's vocabulary is to create a list in a Word file or other text editor, each word on its own line. Save it as a text file. Then go to **DragonBar/ Vocabulary/Import list of words or phrases** and a Wizard will guide you through the process.

To improve Dragon's accuracy go to **DragonBar/Vocabulary/Learn from specific documents.**

You will then be able to browse your documents or folders that contain names, words, or even phrases that you want Dragon to learn. Similarly, you can go to the same Vocabulary menu and select **Learn from sent emails**, which will activate the same sort of process.

Note that Dragon's vocabulary has the names of many well-known people and places already built in. When I dictated the names of such famous composers as Beethoven, Mozart, Berlioz and Gershwin, Dragon recognized them, as well as such legendary personalities as Sinatra, Astaire, Presley, Roosevelt, Nixon, and yes, even Kardashian. Also, such exotic places as Ghana, Kazakhstan, Kuwait, Liechtenstein, Sri Lanka, and Uganda. So before you go through the process of adding a name, search for it in the Vocabulary Editor or just try dictating it to determine if it is already in Dragon's vocabulary.

Choose Your Dragon

As I mentioned earlier, Dragon's manufacturer, Nuance, has regrettably discontinued its NaturallySpeaking software, but it is still available through third-party suppliers. Having used NaturallySpeaking 13 Premium extensively, I believe that it will suit the needs of most users. The two major downsides to acquiring this program now are: Nuance's technical support for NaturallySpeaking will no longer be available as of January, 2019; also, Nuance states that NaturallySpeaking is not compatible with Microsoft Office 365 (and, presumably, later versions to come).

NaturallySpeaking 13 Premium is available three ways: (1) As a CD, boxed with an adequate USB headset; (2) as a CD without the headset; (3) by download. The least expensive source I've come across is eBay where, at this writing, sellers are pricing the CD as low as around $45 (some sellers including the headset) and downloads at about $15. Amazon prices range from $53 to $84.

NaturallySpeaking 13 Home is the entry-level version. I have never used this edition, but I imagine that it does a good job of converting spoken words into written words. However, it lacks some of the Premium edition's functions, as follows: the ability to transcribe recorded files; playback and text-to-speech, that enable you to hear typed material; the ability to import and export custom word lists and user profiles; and speech recognition capability when using Excel and PowerPoint. Also, it does not come with a headset. Prices for the CD are currently $15 on eBay and $29 on Amazon.

Home 15 is Nuance's replacement for the NaturallySpeaking 13 Home edition. The new Home 15 uses the same "Deep Learning" technology as the pricier Professional Individual 15, which, according to Nuance, provides better adaptability to the user's vocabulary. Home 15 also has Dragon's playback mode that allows you to listen to your transcribed speech in your own voice. However, it will not transcribe recorded files. Of course, as a currently produced program, Home 15 can be purchased from Nuance with their 30-day return privilege and 90-day free customer support. Nuance's price is $150 and right now Amazon's price is nearly the same at $148. I did not see any offers on eBay, but they will probably appear in time.

Professional Individual 15 is part of Nuance's top-end series. Priced at $300, it performs similarly to NaturallySpeaking, but with some added features. (For details, see "NaturallySpeaking vs Professional Individual" later in this book.)

Tutorials

Dragon has a built-in tutorial that can be accessed from **DragonBar/Help**. Nuance also provides free documentation on its website: support.nuance.com. There you can download user guides, workbooks, and cheat sheets (listing various commands), and you can watch instructional videos on various topics. As mentioned previously, YouTube is another source for instructional videos by Nuance presenters as well as Dragon users. In addition, Nuance offers a tutorial on DVD for about $30.

Nuance's user guide for NaturallySpeaking 13 is quite comprehensive – currently 259 pages in length – covering the program's installation and operational functions. The workbook for this program, at less than half the length of the user guide, obviously doesn't cover as much territory, but it encourages active reader participation with brief assignments designed to aid in the learning process. I suggest that the prospective user of NaturallySpeaking 13 download the user guide, workbook, and cheat sheet to gain an optimum understanding of the program's various functions

At this writing, there is no user guide for Professional Individual 15, but there is a workbook and cheat sheet

Unfortunately, all of the aforementioned literature is silent on details for uploading recorded dictation into the computer and then getting Dragon to transcribe it. However, you'll find that information right here, in my product review of the Sony ICD-PX440 digital recorder and my product comparison of NaturallySpeaking and Professional Individual.

You can also access Nuance's technical support for their current products. It's free during the first 90 days following product registration. After the 90-day period, the charge per question is $19.95 through a phone call and $9.95 through a web-based ticketing system.

Tutorials from other sources will be found in the Appendix.

Choose Your Accessories

Mic types. Depending on how much you use Dragon, you might be spending a lot of time dictating into a mic, so it's important to choose the types that work best for you. (That's right – *types*. You could well find, as I have, that different types of mics are preferable for different applications. More about that later.) Dragon can be made to work with a mic that's built into your laptop, but its quality might not be good enough for accurate transcriptions.

If you need to buy a mic, your first decision might be whether to choose a stationary mic on a stand or a headset. An obvious advantage of a stationary mic over a headset is that it is not clamped to your head and therefore does not cause even minimal discomfort. The disadvantage is that you have to keep your body in one position while dictating in order for the mic to properly pick up your voice.

One way to give yourself more mobility is to purchase a scissor-type or boom-type stand that allows the mic to be easily moved in various directions. Amazon sells a number of models starting at $14.

Headsets. I have tried three different types of headsets for dictation with Dragon – wired, wireless, and Bluetooth, each with its own benefits and drawbacks.

Wired headset. The main advantage of a wired headset is that it is bone simple – no buttons to push, no battery to keep charged – just a cable that connects directly to your computer. And you get one at no extra cost with some packages of NaturallySpeaking 13 Premium (but not with the basic Home edition). The obvious disadvantage is that it tethers you to the computer. This might work well for a lot of users, but I'm the type who gets up and down a lot and I found that repeatedly removing and replacing the headset was a nuisance, along with the fact that the cable often got entangled with my rolling chair. However, I acquired a wired headset for use with my recorder, and it is reviewed later on.

Wireless vs Bluetooth headset. What, you might wonder, is the difference between a wireless headset and a Bluetooth headset? It's a logical question, because both types are wireless and both types use Bluetooth technology. However, the regular wireless system has its Bluetooth component built into a docking stand that gets its power from a standard wall socket (which, in turn, powers the headset's battery) and therefore cannot be used beyond its range of about 300 feet.

By contrast, a Bluetooth headset has everything encapsulated in the headset itself and therefore can be used anywhere with a Bluetooth-enabled device. It has a range of about 30 feet for dictating directly to your computer

I've explored the other differences in the reviews that follow, and these products are all compatible with Dragon. For a comprehensive list of Dragon-compatible headsets, recorders, and other equipment – including their accuracy ratings – go to http://support.nuance.com/compatibility/Search.asp?PRO=DNS&CID=7. However, be aware that this list is not up-to-date and some of the current recorders, manufactured by Sony, Olympus, Philips, and others, could well be compatible with Dragon even though they do not appear on the list.

Product Review:

Dragon Bluetooth Headset

I purchased from Nuance what they refer to as a Dragon Bluetooth headset but is actually a Plantronics Calisto II. Nuance lists it for $150 but a pop-up banner offered 20% off "if I ordered within the next 20 minutes" (standard hype) so my total cost was $120 plus $10 shipping. However, during its ubiquitous sales events Nuance has offered it for as little as $100 plus shipping, so getting the best price on this and just about everything else Nuance sells depends on your patience and persistence.

The headset is held in place by a hook that fits (more or less) over the ear and a pear-shaped receiver bud that can be maneuvered, with some persuasion, into the opening of the ear canal. I was never able to put this device on without an annoying amount of twisting and pressing. What's more – and this will apply to only a limited number of users – I wear hearing aids and had to remove one of them each time I used the headset, to make room for the receiver bud.

The headset has two controls – a sliding on/off switch to wake it up and a pushbutton to activate the system. The latter requires a sequence of presses that works either the first time or eventually. The battery cannot be charged while the headset is in use and there is no indicator to show how much charge remains in the battery. Therefore, I did a lot of recharging so as not to run out of juice while dictating. To put it mildly, this headset was not a joy to use and I returned it. Nevertheless, I'm giving it 3 stars because it has additional uses for those with Bluetooth-enabled smartphones and other devices.

Product Review:
Jabra Pro 930 UC Cordless Headset

I purchased the Jabra PRO 930 UC through Amazon for $130. This system can be used in either a headband or ear hook configuration. I much prefer the headband, which is lightweight, reasonably comfortable, and sets up easily. One cable is plugged into house current, another into a USB port in your computer. Operation of the system is simple: When not in use, keep the headset on the docking stand, which will recharge its battery as needed whenever the computer is on. An icon on the charging stand indicates when the battery is charging and when battery power is low. To activate the system, double-click a multifunction button on the headset. There are three other buttons: receiver volume up, volume down, and mic mute.

The manufacturer claims that the system's range is up to 325 feet, but I haven't used it any further from my computer than my favorite easy chair, which is about 20 feet away.

Jabra's product literature states that the PRO 930 works with softphones, such as Skype, but I haven't tried that. The manufacturer provides free tech support by telephone, and as far as I can tell, this support has no time limitation.

The Jabra Pro 930 is the headset I use on a daily basis.

Alternative. Nuance offers a free Remote Microphone App that enables you to dictate into a compatible iPhone, iPad, or iPod, using a Wi-Fi network.

The Many Benefits of a Recorder

A compatible digital recorder gives you the freedom to harness the major benefits of Dragon wherever you are. Digital recorders are a major technological advance over the microcassette tape recorders of the past. They have no moving parts, no tape to get snarled up, and they provide internal storage for a lot of dictation – even more with the addition of a Micro SD card. Nuance publishes on their website a list of digital recorders that are compatible with Dragon, including an estimate of each recorder's accuracy for transcription purposes. Unfortunately, Nuance's website is unnecessarily complicated to navigate, but if you type the following very long string into your browser's search bar you should get right to the list: support.nuance.com/compatibility/Search.asp?PRO=DNS&CID=7.

Prices of digital recorders range from $40 to $500. I am quite satisfied with my Sony ICD-PX440 recorder that has Nuance's highest accuracy rating and can be purchased for as low as $55. You'll find a review of this unit later in this book.

For a writer especially, a recorder offers many benefits. One never knows when inspiration might strike, so I slip my compact recorder into a pocket almost every time I go out. Even when I'm visiting a doctor I'll try to find an isolated seat in the waiting room, knowing that the term "waiting" has real significance in a medical facility.

If I have a manuscript that's in the editing stage, I'll bring a printed copy and will hand-write brief edits, but if I come to a place where I want to make a lengthier change,

I'll write, for example, "Insert A" where the change is to go, then I'll dictate "Insert A," followed by the new material. If an idea for a short story occurs to me, I'll dictate an outline for it – or, if I already have the outline I'll dictate at least part of the story. Thus, my waiting time becomes far more productive than leafing through old issues of National Geographic.

I imagine that some good ideas have come to you from out of the blue while you're out and about, and being able to reach into your pocket and record them could give you a considerable head start on getting those ideas into finished form.

The recorder is ideal for travel articles or personal journals where, for example, your impressions of a walk through a rainforest could be recorded on the spot. In fact, in many situations, an entire draft can be completed while you are having the experience.

Think of the many instances where a laptop or even a pad and pen would not be nearly as convenient as a small digital recorder. In the past, the drawback to using a recorder was the inevitable need to sit at the computer and laboriously transcribe your dictation, but today's Dragon does that work for you.

Another use for a recorder is to dictate notes while you are viewing research material, an e-book, or anything else on your computer screen. What's more, a recorder is a great tool for memorizing a speech, which permits better eye contact with the audience than one that is being read. As a public speaker and actor, I find that recording a speech or dialogue and then playing it back repeatedly (while riding in the car, for example) is extremely helpful for memorization.

I also find that simply having a recorder with me is an open invitation to use it. Its very presence gets my "writing brain" in gear. You might have the same experience.

Here's a way that the combination of a recorder and Dragon can be expanded to include other people you are close to: I believe that everyone should strongly consider writing a memoir for the benefit of family and friends. You don't need to be a writer by profession or avocation – anyone can do it, especially with the aid of a recorder, and I expand on this subject in the essay titled *Everyone Should Write a Memoir!* in the Appendix. Children should also be encouraged to keep some sort of journal – and who knows, doing so might lead some of them to develop into writers!

You can use that small portable recorder in other ways as well. If your GPS won't take you there (or if you don't have a GPS) you can dictate step-by-step directions, then play them back while you're enroute to your destination. If you've left your car in a large parking lot or on an unfamiliar city street, you can record a description of the surroundings that will help you find it again. There are other brief reminders, such as a security code you can hide, unidentified, in the recorder's memory. Let your imagination help you discover additional uses for this handy tool.

A limitation of the recorder is that you can't use it in a public place where you are likely to annoy those around you – that is, if you have the consideration for other people that seems to be lacking in many cell phone talkers.

Another downside of dictating into a recorder is that you don't see your words appearing on the computer screen in real time for immediate editing. But that's a small price to pay, and I have become so accustomed to using the recorder that I often do so at home, just to get away from my desktop computer.

For example, I am dictating these very words while stretched out in a reclining chair on my back porch, which has a commanding view of a beautiful lake about 15 yards away, complete with various species of birds that swoop about as they catch their fish dinners. One might argue that this is a distraction and therefore not ideally conducive to productivity, but it works for me and whether or not you have a lake in your backyard, any environment that's pleasurable and quiet might keep your creative juices flowing.

Yet another benefit applies to those who are technologically challenged, busy, or just plain lazy. If you are such a person, you can enjoy the advantages of Dragon without having to learn to use it. Simply dictate into the recorder, hand it to a Dragon-savvy assistant, and take a well-deserved nap.

Product Review:

Sony ICD-PX440 Digital Recorder

This recorder is compact (4.5" x 1.5" x 0.8") and lightweight (about 2.5 oz. including two AAA alkaline batteries) so it fits into my pocket handily. Note that this model is no longer in production but is still available from third-party vendors. More details at the end of this review.

The IC-PX440 can accommodate up to 96 hours of recordings with its built-in 4 GB flash memory and it also has a Micro SD expansion slot for additional recording time. There are ports for an auxiliary headphone and a microphone. A Track Mark function enables you to bookmark places in your recording for quick access. There are recording settings designated as Meeting, Lecture,

Voice Notes, Interview, and Music. A Hold function disables the control buttons so they won't be activated inadvertently. A VOR (Voice Operated Recording) function causes the unit to record only when you speak; when you stop, the recorder goes into Pause mode. However, enabling the VOR function can result in a seriously garbled transcription by Dragon. Therefore, it's better to use the Record button, which toggles between Record and Pause each time you press it.

The IC-PX440 has a couple of useful features of the older tape recorders I've not seen before in a digital recorder: adding material to a file that has already been completed and over-writing parts of a completed file.

The batteries maintain their charge under considerable use.

Following is the process I use to upload my dictation from the Sony recorder to my computer. (Other models might upload by a different procedure.) Using its built-in USB plug I connect the recorder to my computer, which causes the dictation to be uploaded automatically.

I open Dragon and select the user profile I created for use with the recorder. Next, I go to the **DragonBar/Tools/Transcribe Recording**. From the **Transcribe** window that appears I click the **Browse** button and a list appears of all of the files that are in the recorder's memory. Each file is named according to the date on which the recording was made, so if, for example, my last dictation was on October 12, 2018, the file would be identified as 161012001 (year, month, day, file number for that day). If I dictated a second file on that date, its ID would be 161012002, and so on. I select the file or files I want to transcribe by double-clicking on the appropriate

ID(s). Using the Shift or Control key I can select multiple files and they will be transcribed in sequence, which saves a lot of time and effort.

Other details of the transcription process will be found later in the Product Comparison *NaturallySpeaking 13 vs Professional Individual 15.*

In sum, the Sony ICD-PX440 is a high-quality little unit that is convenient to carry and does its job very well.

As I mentioned at the beginning of this review, this particular model is no longer being produced by Sony but as of this writing it is being offered by a number of sellers on eBay at about $35 for used units to about $60 and up for new units.

Sony is currently producing several different digital recorder models, but there is some confusion (at least, in my mind) as to which of them are compatible with Dragon and – even more important – available for purchase. For example, on Sony.com the only model that the manufacturer states is Dragon-compatible is the ICD-UX 530, but I could not find it for sale anywhere and neither could Sony.

On the other hand, there is no mention on Sony's website that the ICD-UX 560BLK is Dragon-compatible but one of the users in his review on Walmart.com states that it is. Their price is $80.

Using Any Old Recorder

If you don't want to spend money on a compatible digital recorder you can try using any other recorder that you might already own. After you've completed your dictation, simply play it back with your mic close to the recorder's speaker and there's a good likelihood that Dragon will transcribe it almost as if you were dictating live into the mic. Yes, that will save you the cost of buying a compatible digital recorder, but you'll pay a price in terms of extra time and effort.

Tip: The above low-tech method might also work with one of Dragon's Home editions, that don't allow uploading of recorded dictation. (The procedure did not work well for me using the free speech recognition programs, but you could try it for yourself.)

When dictating into a recorder, you can use familiar punctuation commands such as **comma, period**, **exclamation point**, **New Line**, **New Paragraph**, **Open Paren**, **Close Paren**, and the various **Caps** commands. Also, you can insert symbols by dictating their names – for example, "ampersand" for **&**, "at sign" for **@**, and "pound sign" for **#**.

Product Review:
Andrea NC-181VM Headset

★★★★★

I bought this headset for use with my Sony digital recorder, mainly for the purpose of hands-free dictating while driving. (I'll get to the safety issue of dictating while driving at the end of this review.) Before I got this headset, I tried a couple of lapel mics. One of them, a Sony ECM CS3, produced good results in a quiet environment, but the road sounds that were transmitted by my great-but-noisy Mazda 3 resulted in a serious degradation of Dragon accuracy.

Then I received a suggestion from Scott Baker, whose tutorials on Dragon I review in the Appendix. He recommended two Andrea Electronics headsets – one mono, one stereo – that have noise-canceling mics. I purchased the mono version from Amazon for $19. (Incidentally, by now you might have noticed that I mention Amazon frequently as a source for purchases. I do this simply because, like a gazillion others, I often buy from them. I receive no compensation or special discounts and, to my regret, I don't even own any Amazon stock.)

The Andrea headset has an adjustable headband, mute switch and volume control. There is just one earphone, with a temple pad on the opposite side. This arrangement is beneficial for driving, as it keeps the uncovered ear open to traffic sounds. The headband is comfortable and the mic boom is easily adjusted to a variety of positions. Best of all, the noise-canceling mic overcomes road noise to provide about as much Dragon accuracy as I normally get in a completely quiet environment.

I also use this headset for the fortunately rare occasions when I have to fall back on the parroting technique, described earlier, for salvaging a recording that has befuddled Dragon.

Safety disclaimer: Nothing in the above product review should be interpreted as a recommendation that you dictate while driving. That is a personal choice, and bear in mind that any activity unrelated to one's driving – whether it's taking a sip of coffee, having a cell phone chat, or even conversing with a passenger – can be something of a distraction. I am not a safety expert, but common sense tells me that when I am doing any activity – including dictation – that is not directly connected to my driving, I need to be aware of the potential for distraction and not allow my attention to stray from what is happening on the road. Also, if there is a need for extra attention, such as heavy traffic, navigation, passing through a school zone, etc., I stop whatever else I'm doing and concentrate 100% on driving.

Product Comparison:
NaturallySpeaking Premium 13
vs
Professional Individual 15

One interesting feature of Professional Individual comes into play when you are recording a speaker for whom there is no user profile. During the process of transcribing any uploaded recording, you are prompted to choose between your own user profile and "Someone Else." Transcribing "Someone Else" works well if you have recorded, say, a podcast or a YouTube soundtrack, where you can control the speaker's volume. But if you are recording a live speaker at a meeting or classroom you are not likely to get a usable transcription unless the speaker is close to your recorder's mic and is projecting at a good volume.

Of course, transcribing someone else's speech would normally require that you add punctuation when editing, but during the transcription process you can check a box **Automatically add commas and periods**, which performs that function for you. It works fairly well but not perfectly.

At this point, I want to reiterate that I do not attempt to evaluate all of the Dragon programs' features. Instead, I focus primarily on their empowerment of the user to create documents and correspondence more easily and more productively by dictating rather than by typing.

Both NaturallySpeaking and Professional Individual provide the user with additional capabilities, such as dictating entries into Excel and navigating the Web by voice commands. You'll find details on these features in other tutorials, but for now, here are some extra functions that have been incorporated into Professional Individual 15, as stated in Nuance's promotional material:

- *Easily create or import powerful commands to automate time-consuming tasks and reduce time associated with document creation.*
- *Easily import/export custom commands or multiple vocabularies, set permissions on custom commands and more.*
- *Dragon will now monitor a specific directory to automatically launch transcription and provides an audio file for deferred correction.*

It's worth noting that if you are already using NaturallySpeaking, you can transition easily to Professional Individual – both programs operate similarly.

Which raises the question, how does the speech recognition accuracy of the more expensive Professional Individual compare to that of NaturallySpeaking? In its promotional literature, Nuance claims that Professional Individual 15 has 15% greater out-of-the-box accuracy, which *"comes courtesy of a smarter, next-generation speech engine leveraging Deep Learning technology."*

And what is Deep Learning technology? Here's part of Nuance's explanation as it appears in their blog: *"This allows us to go beyond speaker-independent speech recognition by adapting to each user in a speaker-dependent way... It adapts to the user's active vocabulary by inspecting texts the user has created in the past, both by adding custom words to its active vocabulary and by learning the typical phrases and text patterns the user employs."*

Sounds very impressive, but after more than two years of my almost daily use of Professional Individual 15, including initiation of the program's accuracy enhancing functions, I'm getting roughly the same number and type of errors I experienced with NaturallySpeaking 13.

This includes the context in which words are used, which both programs are supposed to understand. Take, for example, the words **to** and **two** which, of course, sound exactly alike. Dragon is supposed to know which word to transcribe according to the meaning of the sentence that is dictated. Thus, if I dictate "I bought two apples," Dragon should not transcribe that as "I bought **to** apples." But that's what I sometimes get. Also, Dragon (like many real people) gives me the ubiquitous **it's** when the context of the sentence cries out for **its**.

Don't get me wrong, I'm a true believer in Dragon, but I also believe in what a former US President said in another context: "Trust but verify" – in this case, verify by very careful proofreading, especially if writing is your day job.

Let's move on to the process of transcribing your own recorded text, and, as I mentioned in my review of the Sony recorder, each program does this in a different way. NaturallySpeaking will send the transcribed text quickly and directly to a document you're working on, wherever you have placed your cursor. You can watch the transcription as it's taking place – and as you watch, you can decide on any changes you will want to make.

However, you cannot use your computer for any other purpose until the transcription is finished.

By contrast, Professional Individual will not show the transcription until it has been completed, after which a menu gives you a choice of three destinations for the transcribed text: DragonPad, the clipboard, or a stand-alone Word file. You then have to cut and paste the text into the desired document.

Dragon takes one minute to transcribe each minute of recorded material. Therefore, if you have a recorded file that's 25 minutes long it will take Dragon 25 minutes to transcribe it. Meanwhile, Professional Individual allows you to do other work with your computer except for direct dictation, as your mic will be disabled while the transcription process is underway.

There is one important consideration that could weigh heavily in your decision: As I mentioned earlier, Nuance states that NaturallySpeaking 13 is not compatible with Microsoft Office 2016 (also known as Office 365). Presumably, this same compatibility issue will also apply to future editions of Microsoft Office.

If this this does not concern you, I suggest that the main reasons for choosing the pricier Professional Individual would be Nuance's ongoing technical support – no longer available for NaturallySpeaking as of January 1, 2019 – and/or you have a need for one or more of Professional Individual's unique features.

In addition, Professional Individual is available in specialized versions configured for the legal and medical professions.

I am not privy to Nuance's plans, if any, for an eventual direct replacement of NaturallySpeaking 13, but I hope that we will soon see an equivalent program in terms of features and price -- whether from Nuance or another software provider – so that consumers will once again have a suitable range of choices.

Summing Up

I hope that the information in this book will motivate you to try speech recognition software and discover how much easier it is to write by speaking instead of typing. And I urge you to give it a *good* try. That is, don't get discouraged if you find the process of dictation challenging at first. Just turn your thoughts into words and then let the words flow – you can easily correct any mistakes later. And as you become more comfortable with dictation, I believe that you will find it enjoyable as well as rewarding.

The easiest way to get started is to try one or more of the free speech recognition programs described earlier. That might be all you need. But bear in mind that one of the Dragon programs – particularly NaturallySpeaking 13 Premium or Professional Individual 15 – will very likely require less correcting and will give you greater capability, especially with the added benefits you can receive if you use a compatible digital recorder.

The choice is yours to make. But the first decision is to get started.

Oh, but before you do, please read the few remaining pages of this book. The Appendix has some useful information for you and I sincerely hope that my essay *Everyone Should Write a Memoir!* will inspire you to embark on a project that will give lasting gratification to you, your family, and your friends.

Appendix

Additional resources. *Dragon NaturallySpeaking for Dummies.* The 4th Edition focuses on NaturallySpeaking 13. It is written by Stephanie Diamond in the typical breezy, highly readable Dummies style. The 5th Edition is titled *Dragon Professional Individual for Dummies,* also written by Stephanie Diamond and it deals with the original Professional Individual 14. (A 6th Edition, presumably covering the current Professional Individual 15, had been scheduled but at this writing its publication was canceled.)

The Writer's Guide to Training Your Dragon by Scott Baker. In this fact- and opinion-filled book, the author provides considerable detail about software and such hardware as computers and mics. I recommend this book even though I take issue with some of the author's positions. For example, he advises his readers to "steer clear" of wireless headsets and he bolsters his position by stating, *"There are some very good quality wireless headphones out there, but they tend to cost a fortune and you would be likely to get equally good, if not better, quality from a wired microphone costing a tenth of the price."* Let's examine that claim. Baker recommends the Blue Snowball Ice wired microphone that currently sells for $49 on Amazon. This is hardly a tenth of the price of my Jabra 930 Pro UC wireless headset that works fine with Dragon (and other speech recognition programs) and is currently available for about $128. On the whole, though, Baker's book is filled with useful information and tips on dictating with Dragon. As icing on the cake, there is a link that provides free access to Baker's training videos. *The*

Writer's Guide to Training Your Dragon is available both as a Kindle e-book and a paperback. Baker has also authored a shorter companion e-book, *Quick Cheats for Writing with Dragon*, which, the last time I looked, was available on Amazon for free. But don't be misled by its freebie status – this book is chock-full of valuable tips regarding the selection of equipment for use with Dragon.

There are books by other authors on dictation techniques in general, but as of this writing, my book is the only publication I'm aware of that covers Dragon Professional Individual 15 and, incidentally, compares it with other Dragon products.

Here's a totally different type of resource: Consider joining a Toastmasters club in your area. The main purpose of Toastmasters is to help people improve their skills in public speaking and this could likely help many people become more confident and fluent in the dictation process.

More than that, the speeches, which can be on virtually any subject the speaker chooses, are gently and positively critiqued on their content and delivery. Toastmasters is a worldwide organization and you can find a club in your area on toastmasters.org. Visitors are always welcome.

I have been a Toastmaster for more than 15 years and find my participation to be a constantly rewarding experience.

Finally, I offer the following essay for you and those you love.

Everyone Should Write a Memoir!
And Voice Typing Can Help

Write a memoir. It doesn't matter whether you are a beginning writer or a seasoned pro – or even if you don't consider yourself to be a writer at all. Write a memoir to present the gift of your inner self to your family, friends, and perhaps a wider audience. You might publish only a few dozen copies for a very limited distribution, but then again, a really compelling story could be the beginning of a new career.

A basic writer's axiom advises you to "write what you know," and what could be more familiar to you than an episode in your own life? And here's what makes it so special: A memoir can give your loved ones a greater insight into who you are and how you got to become the person you are – your thoughts, your feelings, your adventures through life, and the things you learned along the way. And you don't have to wait until your sunset years; you can write a memoir at any age. You can do it now.

Let me be clear as to what I mean by "memoir." Some people might consider "memoir" as being synonymous with "autobiography." Not entirely. While an autobiography is a very extensive memoir, usually taking in the entire life of the subject, a memoir can also be just a small nugget of that person's existence – a series of reminiscences, or even a single recollection. So it's not that daunting a task.

Even so, how valuable would such a memoir be to others? Well, think of somebody who is important to you – your mother, father, grandparent, friend – and even though you've known that person for years, you sense that there are aspects of that person's life that you don't know about and wish you did. Not necessarily skeletons in the closet, but – wouldn't it be fun to know that Grandma always wanted to be a trapeze artist, but somehow never got around to it?

My best friend since high school was, for most of his adult life, a sales executive whose high-powered drive enabled him to found and manage several insurance companies and later become a director of various financial institutions. I thought I knew him pretty well, but I was astonished when he sent me a book of sensitive and lovely poetry that he had written! To my everlasting sorrow, Frank is gone now, but through his poetry I saw an aspect of him I had never suspected, and my respect and admiration for my friend became even greater.

Well, you might not be a secret poet, or even a wannabe trapeze artist, but aren't there some unrevealed parts of you that you wouldn't mind sharing – in fact, that you might be a little proud of?

Write it down. Write your memoir. One of the easiest ways to get it done is to use Dragon and a compatible recorder, as described in this book. Go to a quiet place, turn your recorder on, and speak your recollections. Don't worry about grammar or punctuation – just talk. You can fix it later. If it would help get the thoughts flowing, sit down with someone you feel comfortable with and start chatting about a topic for your memoir.

Regardless of where your memoir begins, it can take on a life of its own – because it is, after all, the life of your own. Write your memoir for yourself and for the ones you love. And maybe for some great-great-grandchildren you will never know – but through your memoir, they will get to know you.

Also by Keith Connes

Know Your Airplane!

The GPS & Nav/Comm Buyer's Guide

How to Meet a Lovely Asian Girl
  ... and Bring Her Home!

Get me a Schoolgirl!

Surprising Turns!

Not Your Everyday Memoir!

Romance with a ROBOT

  Plus 5 Other Exciting Robot Stories

About the Author

Keith Connes has accumulated a lot of writing mileage. He started getting paid for his words at age 20 and at this writing he is 92, so you can easily do the math. Yes, he can still remember where he left the car keys – well, most of the time – and what's more, his wife is age 30. This last is mentioned, not to boast of his romantic prowess, which is dubious at best, but rather to plug his book titled *How to Meet a Lovely Asian Girl ... and Bring Her Home!* readily available on Amazon. It is a true account of his many amorous escapades, starting at age 80 (when he should have known better) and taking place in Thailand and the Philippines.

Also in the book is a lot of realistic information on dealing with the eccentricities of the Immigration Service – especially useful for those who might like to venture overseas and do likewise, hopefully at a more sensible age.

Earlier in life, while in servitude as a TV and radio commercial writer for several major ad agencies, Connes took up flying to get his mind off his work and eventually became an aviation writer, editor, and book publisher. Over the years he has written approximately 150 magazine articles and several books, one of which was likely the first consumer guide on GPS navigation.

While conducting his excursions to Asia, he combated the boredom of the long flights by bringing a laptop and writing short stories on it. Long after the overseas flights, he is still writing short stories and there are currently three collections of them on Kindle. One of them is definitely not family oriented. Its title, *Get Me a Schoolgirl!*, says it all. The other two, *Surprising Turns!* and

Romance with a Robot, are somewhat less – er, graphic – but still have their intense moments.

During all of his adult life, Connes has also enjoyed pleasurable sidelines as an actor, singer, and public speaker. Some of these experiences have been recounted in his mostly humorous grab-bag of recollections *Not Your Everyday Memoir!*

Full disclosure: Author bios are either written by the author or are based on information provided by the author and, it follows, most of them are completely self-serving. This bio is no exception.